4/28/11

Kristen,

God has given you a gift.
Use it to inspire others
like you have inspired me
in so many ways.

You will be an amazing "coach"!

Happiness for you always, my friend,

Shelley

Today, I will
begin changes that will
influence the shape of my life
for years to come.

Blue Mountain Arts®

New and Best-Selling Titles

Be Filled with Faith, by Rachel Snyder

Daring to Be Ourselves
from Interviews by Marianne Schnall

A Daughter Is Life's Greatest Gift

For You, My Soul Mate, by Douglas Pagels

I Thanked God for You Today, by Donna Fargo

Irish Inspirations

Keep Believing in Yourself and Your Dreams

The Love Between a Mother and Daughter Is Forever

The Path to Success Is Paved with Positive Thinking
by Wally Amos with Stu Glauberman

The Promises of Marriage

A Son Is Life's Greatest Gift

The Strength of Women

Take Time for You
by M. Butler and D. Mastromarino

To My Daughter with Love on the Important Things in Life
by Susan Polis Schutz

To My One True Love
by Susan Polis Schutz

To My Son with Love
by Susan Polis Schutz

Today, I Will...
by James Downton, Jr.

Today, I Will...

Words to Inspire Positive Life Changes

James Downton, Jr.

Blue Mountain Press™
Boulder, Colorado

Library of Congress Catalog Card Number: 2009015054
ISBN: 978-1-59842-424-9

▌and Blue Mountain Press are registered in U.S. Patent and Trademark Office.
Certain trademarks are used under license.

Printed in China.
Second Printing: 2010

✪ This book is printed on recycled paper.

This book is printed on archival quality, white felt, 110 lb. paper. This paper has been specially produced to be acid free (neutral pH) and contains no groundwood or unbleached pulp. It conforms with the requirements of the American National Standards Institute, Inc., so as to ensure that this book will last and be enjoyed by future generations.

Library of Congress Cataloging-in-Publication Data

Downton, James, 1938-
  Today, I will— : words to inspire positive life changes / James Downton, Jr.
    p. cm.
  ISBN 978-1-59842-424-9 (trade pbk. : alk. paper) 1. Conduct of life. 2. Spiritual life. 3. Change (Psychology) I. Title.
  BJ1581.2.D69 2009
  170′.44—dc22
                                                    2009015054

Blue Mountain Arts, Inc.
P.O. Box 4549, Boulder, Colorado 80306

Contents

6   A Letter to You, the Reader

9   Today, I Will…

10 Make This a Good Day

12 Nurture Valued Relationships

14 Notice the Riches in My Life

16 Appreciate Simple Pleasures

18 Be Open to Change

20 Approach Life with a
    Lighter Heart

22 Have Fun

24 Enjoy Nature

26 Be Amazed

28 Seek Peace

30 Slow Down

32 Recharge My Batteries

34 Relax

36 Live at My Own Pace

38 Practice Grace
    and Acceptance

40 Shift My Perspective

42 Express Gratitude and
    Encouragement

44 Make a Difference

46 See How I Have Improved
    with Age

48 Be Proud of Who I Am

50 Recall Good Memories

52 Reject Fear

54 Take Risks

56 Tap into My Creativity

58 Revise My Life Story

60 Learn Something

62 Ask for Help

64 Pursue My Dreams

66 Be Kind to Myself

68 Not Take Things Personally

70 Nurture Community

72 Communicate and Listen
    with Compassion

74 Let Go and Forgive

76 Prevent Problems

78 Examine My Life Direction

80 Be Flexible

82 Cultivate Wisdom

84 Choose My Thoughts Carefully

86 Seek Balance

88 Love Myself

90 Create My Ideal Day

92 Thrive

A Letter to You, the Reader

Gardeners grow beautiful and bountiful gardens through hard work and patience. They improve the soil, prune, weed, and water until their vision is realized. Imagine being a life gardener, where you cultivate yourself with the same determination. With effort and patience, you would evolve in positive ways until you bloomed as a person. In bloom, you would be happier, more creative, more fulfilled, and have greater peace of mind. In this more positive state, your relationships and life would flourish. You would see wonderful things grow up around you because of who you had become. Your life garden would be beautiful and bountiful.

The simple thoughts in this book are life-gardening tools to help nurture your personal growth. They create awareness, open up new choices, and pave the way for more positive thoughts, feelings, and relationships. Practice, like weeding, is hard, but it is what produces enduring changes.

Use the book as you wish. You can make your way slowly from cover to cover, working with a thought for a day or a week. You can randomly open the book and choose a thought to inspire a change of mind or heart. You can quietly meditate on the thoughts, keep a journal of insights and changes they have inspired, or do both. You can work through the book with a friend to share discoveries and help each other make constructive changes.

When I was in my late thirties, a question suddenly flashed into my mind that changed my life. It was a simple question: how far can I develop as a person over the remaining years of my life? Inspired by this guiding question, I started doing life-gardening work to make positive changes in my conditioned ways of thinking, feeling, and relating to others. Over thirty years later, I am still doing that inner work while also lending a hand to others who are determined to grow.

How far can you develop as a person over the remaining years of your life? What is the life-gardening work that you will want to do? How will you use the simple thoughts in this book as tools in your life-gardening effort?

Good gardening,

Jim

I will use positive thoughts to create more happiness and success in my life.

Today, I Will...

The past is past and this day is new, so a fresh opportunity for change presents itself to me now. Today, I will listen to the heartfelt voice in me saying, "Notice and appreciate the goodness in people. Live from the goodness within yourself."

When we live more fully in the present, we awaken the mind to the little miracles of life. Today, I will live each moment as if it were a unique masterpiece as fascinating as a great work of art. By keeping my attention on "now," I will get to smell, touch, hear, see, and taste the daily miracles I fail to notice when I am lost in the past or preoccupied with plans for the future.

Today, I Will...
Make This a Good Day

A "good day" lies within our power to create. Today, I will make this a good day by encouraging and being kind to myself. I will improve this day for others by giving them my attention, compassion, and support. By setting out to create a good day, I will see how much power for good lies within me.

How we focus our minds is crucial. Today, I will focus on what I have, rather than what is absent. I will focus on what is working, rather than what is not working. When gazing at a rosebush, I can focus on the thorns or the flowers. For today, I will see and celebrate the flowers.

We can ruin a perfectly good day after something goes wrong or the weather fails to suit us. We make up the thought "This is going to be a bad day," then for the rest of the day, we are determined to prove it. Today, I will think about how I spoil perfectly good days. Do good days become bad when an interaction goes wrong or I feel stuck trying to solve a problem? By seeing how I ruin perfectly good days, I have the choice to put a stop to it.

We often get back from others what we have given them. If people treat us badly, it may be because we have treated them badly. If people love us, it may be because we have treated them in loving ways. Today, I will explore how my treatment of others has affected their treatment of me. What I learn may cause me to celebrate myself or change how I treat others.

Today, I Will...
Nurture Valued Relationships

Important connections between people can be eroded by simple neglect. Today, I will be aware of valued relationships I have quit tending. Have I stopped actively cultivating ties with a parent, grandparent, sister, brother, child, or friend? Who would welcome special time with me, a telephone call, or a heartfelt letter? By renewing my ties with others, I will feel renewed.

Each of us can easily offer help to others. Today, I will reach out to help people I encounter with a kind word, with optimism, with encouragement. I will feel a spirit of goodwill enveloping me so that I might serve others without wanting anything in return but the good feeling of having helped.

When we love ourselves, all our relationships work better. Today, I will notice what I like about myself. By discovering what I like, I will create a more affectionate bond with myself. Knowing I am in a more loving relationship with myself, I will approach my other relationships with a more positive spirit.

Two sentences will significantly improve any relationship: "I love you" will deepen it and "I'm sorry" will repair it. Today, I will consider how hard it is for me to speak these words. Am I able to say "I love you" or "I'm sorry" at the appropriate moment? This awareness will help me understand how I can more effectively deepen the love in my relationships and repair them after an argument.

Today, I Will...
Notice the Riches in My Life

Caught up in the effort to make money, we can forget to notice how rich we already are. Today, I will be aware of the many valuable things I have. Who are the people who love me and give my life meaning? What aspects of my life create fun and adventure? As I remember all the riches of my life, I will see how wealthy I really am.

Treasures are everywhere. Today, I am going to notice hidden treasures. Maybe it will be an old man's joy while he retrieves a ball from the street for some young children or savoring the taste of an ice-cream cone. By seeing the small treasures of life, I will receive their riches.

To love and be loved are priceless treasures. Today, I will see what loving and being loved do for me. How do my expressions of love for others nourish them? How does experiencing the love of others nourish me? By noticing the gifts of love, I will see how rich I am.

We can suffer because of our desires and expectations. Today, I will discover how my desires and expectations make me disappointed with life. I will recognize that by wanting life to be a certain way, I create my own suffering by resisting what is. Instead of resisting today, I will dance with my circumstances.

Today, I Will...
Appreciate Simple Pleasures

Simple things can be sources of great happiness. Today, I will savor the simple things that make me happy. Maybe I will enjoy the pleasure of holding a child's hand, smelling a flower, seeing someone smile, drinking a glass of fresh orange juice, or taking a long walk. As I pause to enjoy the simple things of life, I will see how much they contribute to my feelings of happiness.

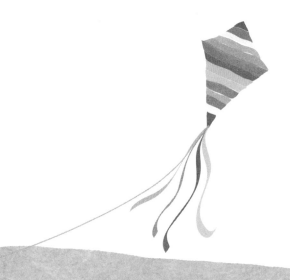

When we look up close at things, we discover the hidden wonders of life. Today, I will carefully look at things I normally fail to notice, like the beauty of reflections in windows, the artful forms of shadows, and the mystery of a fleeting glance from a stranger. By seeing the hidden art of life, I will open a little door of awareness into my daily heaven.

Appreciation is an act of celebration. Today, I will do my best to find something to appreciate about myself, my relationships, each person I meet, and each situation I face. I will feel deeper appreciation for my life and for the many blessings that come my way. This day will be a time for celebration.

Mustard and relish are embellishments that improve the taste of a hot dog. Today, I will add one little embellishment to my life to improve it. Maybe I will decide to start singing in the shower, take myself out to breakfast once a week, or schedule a massage once a month. By adding one little embellishment, I will improve the taste of my life.

Today, I Will...
Be Open to Change

A well-trodden life path can become a safe route we never question. Today, I will spend time questioning the path I have been on. Am I using myself in ways that make my life meaningful? Have I added enough risk to how I am being and living so I can experience my life as a creative adventure? As I explore the path I have been taking today, I will learn what I might change to make it more challenging and interesting.

When warmed by the sun, ice melts and becomes flowing water. Today, I will discover places within myself where I have become hard like ice. Which of my emotions, beliefs, attitudes, or judgments have become too hard? By warming up my heart, I will melt what has hardened in order to increase my ability to flow.

Opportunities for personal growth are present if we listen carefully for their quiet calls. Today, I will listen for their calls from old places, new places, and hidden places. What am I being called to change in myself, my relationships, and my way of living? By responding to a call, I prepare myself to make a change.

A bumper sticker to make us laugh and grow: "Of all the things I have lost, I miss my mind the most." Today, I will identify the parts of my mind I would love to lose. What thoughts and attitudes do I have regularly that undermine me, my relationships, my happiness, and my effectiveness? By knowing what parts of my mind I need to lose, I will discover an opportunity to change.

Today, I Will...
Approach Life with a Lighter Heart

Having a sense of humor adds balance to life. Today, instead of taking life seriously, I will see the humor in what people say and do. In this more playful mood, I will watch this day unfold like a comedy.

Smiling is definitely contagious. Today, I will smile at everyone I see and enjoy the effect when they smile back at me. By smiling together, our inner lights will shine so we can spread a bit of happiness around.

"No" is as good a choice as "yes." Today, I will have the freedom to say "no" without feeling guilty or disappointed in myself. Instead, I will feel an unusual pleasure from the experience of protecting myself. By saying "no," the spirit of freedom will emerge within me like a glorious bloom.

A good laugh is great medicine. Today, I will explore my life with the spirit of a comedian. What am I doing and who am I being that, from a comic's point of view, would be the basis for a good joke? How can I see my life as a silly comedy rather than a soap opera? Instead of life being a bellyache, it will become a source for belly laughs.

Today, I Will...
Have Fun

Playfulness adds the bubbles to life. Today, I will encourage lighthearted fun to bubble up in my interactions with others. As I let myself play, I will reawaken the fun-loving spontaneity I experienced so freely as a child. Instead of life being a proving ground, it will be my playground.

When we hold back our playfulness, we miss the fun in life. Today, I will explore ways to liberate my playful nature. Could I be less serious, less afraid, less cautious, and less concerned about impressing others? By giving my mind more freedom to play, I get to have a lot more fun today.

A soda without the fizz is pretty disappointing. Today, I will explore my fizziness. Where have I lost some of my fizz? Where in my life do I need to add a special fizzy spirit? With greater awareness, I get to create more effervescence today. I will become a soda with a nice bubbly kick.

Joy is the light of happiness turned up. Today, I will cultivate joy within myself. As I turn up my inner light, I will notice how it affects me, others, and my surroundings. I will journey beyond simple happiness to explore the brighter light of joy!

Today, I Will...
Enjoy Nature

We are racing through space on a heavenly planet in an amazing universe. Today, I will renew my spirit by deepening my connection to nature. Maybe I will walk through grass in my bare feet, listen to a stream, or go out late tonight to look up at the stars. I will feel the pulse of nature.

Birds bless us each day with their joyful singing. Today, I will notice their songs as gifts of cheerfulness, playfulness, and hope. Emulating the spirit of birds, I will sing a song of playful optimism today.

A single flower can sometimes speak with more affection than a dozen. Today, I will give a single flower to someone who counts in my life. Selecting the flower with that person in mind, I might choose a daisy, a lily, or a rose. Just think how happy the flower will be to carry my affection.

We are living in a miracle and often fail to notice it. Today, I will live in awe of the miracle of life. I will be in awe of the sun, water, sky, earth, people, flowers, laughter, smiles, and a myriad of other amazing things. I will see the miracle around me.

Today, I Will...
Be Amazed

Amazement appears to the mind that seeks it. Today, I will have the ability to be amazed by the little things I have been failing to notice and the big things I have taken for granted. By creating amazement in the way I see, I will give birth to awe and wonder.

People who look at the ground when they walk fail to see the amazing sky. Today, I will notice which thoughts, problems, and activities most prevent me from seeing what is wonderful about life. Do I get lost in doubt and forget to look for wonder? Do I work so hard to succeed that I fail to see life's little gifts? This awareness will help me create better balance so I can see the ground and the sky and feel happier to be alive.

The inner light of goodness shines in everyone. Today, I will look for that light of goodness in others. I will see the light emerging in their smiles, laughter, playful moments, compassion, and kindness. Seeing the radiant inner light of others, I will turn up the light within myself.

Every sunrise is special in its own way. Today, I will experience this day as unique like a sunrise. What novelties will I notice? What beautiful moments will I see? How will I add my own touches of beauty to this day? Instead of being "just another day," I will make it into something really special.

Today, I Will...
Seek Peace

A peaceful mind arises when we quit
trying so hard to mold life to suit our purposes.
Today, I will stop trying so hard to shape life
to suit me, so I can experience a bit more
peace within myself, with others, and with
my circumstances. Feeling more inner peace,
I will be able see myself and my life in a new
way; not as an overwhelming struggle, but as
something akin to challenging river rapids
that require both balance and courage to
navigate successfully.

Blessed are the peacemakers; they are the healers of social wounds. Today, I will look for opportunities to make peace. Where there is misunderstanding, division, or conflict, I will draw on my creative resources to help heal it. As I seek to make peace between people, I will work from a place of peace within myself.

Eyes are the windows of the soul. Today, I will look deeply into my eyes to see the part of me that already lives in peace. Being in that peace, I will turn to the inner light of my own wholeness so I can hear a quiet voice whisper, "You are loved, always."

When we are at peace, peace grows up around us. Today, I will find ways of being peaceful with myself, other people, and my work. As I cultivate peaceful feelings within myself, I will be sowing seeds of peace all around me.

Today, I Will...
Slow Down

We rush through our days without pausing to really notice. Today, I will stop from time to time to reflect on what I am seeing, what I am doing, who I am being, and what effects I am having on others. In those pauses, I will see opportunities for appreciating and changing the quality of my life.

Going too fast will eventually produce trouble. Today, I will explore where I am going at breakneck speed in my life, which could land me in trouble. Am I doing my work at such a fast pace that its quality is declining? Do I drive my car so fast and myself so hard that the risks are escalating? By noticing where I am going too fast, I will know where to slow down so I can reduce my chances of getting into trouble.

Trying to drive straight on a crooked road is pretty foolish. Today, I will consider where I am trying to plow straight ahead in my life when I should be navigating the curves with care. Where am I forcing my will on circumstances when I could be more flexible, more creative, and wiser?

Impatience is trying to go faster than the speed of life. Today, I will travel at the slower speed of life by not rushing faster than circumstances allow. Instead, I will be accepting and patient with the pace of things. By being more patient, I will attune myself to the natural pace of life. By moving at that slower speed, I will find that I am more contented and more effective.

Today, I Will...
Recharge My Batteries

Feeling dried up and uninspired usually originates in our thinking. Today, I will explore the parts of my life that have lost inspiration and vitality. Seeing what needs to be renewed, I will cultivate a change in my thinking. I will be like a gardener who is determined to revive a withered plant by giving it careful attention, cultivation, nutrients, and water. By gardening myself and my life with a deep desire to change, I will create a period of renewal and inspiration.

Worthless things do not attain value just because we hold on to them. Today, I will become aware of worthless things I have accumulated within my thinking and my life. What thoughts and things could I throw out or give away to reap some nice benefits? I will do some life cleaning today.

A drained person is like a well without water, which is of no use to anyone. Today, I will take steps to restore my energy. Should I take a peaceful walk, lie down for a nap, meditate, or eat a nourishing meal? By pumping energy into my well, I will restore my drive and enthusiasm.

The ability to shift from negative to positive emotions makes us happier and more effective. Today, I will switch to emotions that will serve me. If I start feeling bored, I will shift to excitement. If I begin feeling afraid, I will shift to courage. If I become discouraged, I will shift to hope. By learning to shift from negative to positive emotions, I will increase my chances of attaining greater happiness and success.

Today, I Will...
Relax

When we grip life too hard, living becomes more tense and difficult. Today, I will notice the places in my life where I am creating stress and difficulties by trying too hard. Am I trying too hard to impress others? Am I trying too hard to get my way? As I relax and seek more balance, I will find that living can be easier.

Putting on a pair of slippers is a good remedy for stress. Today, I will experience the good feelings of being in my favorite slippers — relaxed, at ease, and comfortable. When I am facing challenges, I will hear my slippers' quiet voices call out, "Relax, be at ease, feel comfortable." By heeding these words, I will become the remedy for stress.

Taking a vacation is a good way to forget worries. Today, I am going to take a vacation from a problem. Maybe I will take a vacation from worrying about how I look, how smart or interesting I am, how much I have to do, or how a relationship problem is nagging me. I am taking a vacation from a worry today. Taking a break from my problem, I am already feeling better.

A sunflower will turn toward the warm light of the sun. Today, I will turn toward my inner light. I will think within it, act within it, and live within it. Like a sunflower, I will grow from being touched by it.

Today, I Will...
Live at My Own Pace

We are run by time. Today, I will notice time: how I watch it, use it, waste it, and wish I had a lot more of it. I will have a better chance of running time when I start to understand how it runs me.

There are strong pressures on us to perform at high speed and still produce high-quality work. Trying to live up to this expectation can make us feel guilty, stressed out, and miserable. Today, I will not feel guilty for just doing my best under the circumstances. My goal for the day will be to do quality work at a pace that will ensure greater creativity, more effectiveness, and peace of mind.

Living within limits can help us but it can also stifle our creativity. Today, I will think about the limits others impose on me and also the limits I place on myself. With wisdom in mind, which of those limits should I accept? With creativity in mind, which of those limits should I challenge? My answers to these questions will lead me to balance and effectiveness.

Knowing what is valuable is invaluable. Today, I will live as if this were my last day. I will see what is important in my life and what is less significant. This awareness will help me adjust my priorities.

Today, I Will...
Practice Grace and Acceptance

"Grace" is the capacity to see what is already good in life. Today, I will live in grace by noticing the big and little miracles around me. Instead of focusing on my problems and what is missing from my life, I will see the many wonderful things that come my way without my even asking.

Life is what it is — sometimes easy and sometimes difficult — but always challenging. Today, I will accept life for what it is, not as a guaranteed easy ride, but one with unexpected and scary curves and steep drop-offs. Instead of resisting the adventure, I will ride the ups and downs of this day like a teenager who loves the excitement of a roller-coaster ride.

The time in which we live is our fate, while how we handle it is a choice. Today, I will accept my fate as a challenge life has given me. I will explore how I feel about it and new ways to deal with it. Instead of resisting my fate, I will find ways to live creatively within it.

Second best can be quite good. Today, I will explore what I am happy to accept when I cannot get exactly what I want. Am I happy to accept a raise when it is not as high as I had hoped? To enjoy someone's company when I really want that person's love? I will see how accepting second best brings me small treasures.

Today, I Will...
Shift My Perspective

"I have to" is a common expression in our lives. Today, when I hear myself say "I have to," I will replace it with "I get to." I will notice how this simple shift in my thinking changes my relationship to my responsibilities. I will discover how lucky I am to have the ability to take action.

Making small problems into big ones is a source of human misery we can change. Today, I will reduce the size of my biggest problem by viewing it from the perspective of time. Will it be a big problem in one year, in ten years, or toward the end of my life? Seeing my big problem over the long term, it will seem like "small stuff." With a smaller problem, I will have less stress and worry to carry around.

We can shape our moods by managing our minds. Today, I will notice how my bad moods tend to control me rather than the other way around. As an experiment, I will create a good mood today. Do I want to create a cooperative mood, a playful mood, a hopeful mood, or a creative mood? Instead of being at the mercy of my moods, they will bow down to me today.

A fresh outlook arises when we see a problem from several points of view. Today, I will explore a crucial issue in my life from three new perspectives. As I change my viewpoints, I will create new ideas about how to approach the problem.

Today, I Will...
Express Gratitude and Encouragement

There are people we rely on for help. Today, I will see if my reliance on them and my expressions of appreciation are in balance. Whom do I ask to help me on a regular basis? Do I ask too much of them too often? Do I show enough appreciation? By considering balance, I may make a change.

Words have power. They can inspire or hurt. Today, I will watch my words by speaking with mindfulness. The words I speak will elevate, not diminish, the spirits of others.

Receiving gracefully is as important as giving. Today, I will explore how I respond when I receive gifts, compliments, and help from others. Do I thankfully and gracefully accept or put up resistance? By noticing how I respond, I can become more generous in my receiving so others can feel good about giving.

Sweet is the word that offers encouragement. Today, I will speak words of encouragement to myself and others. I will live in the connection between encouragement and determination as they work together to create new life.

Today, I Will...
Make a Difference

Everyone is resourceful. Today, I will identify the personal resources I have been neglecting to use. Am I failing to use my ability to listen carefully? Has my sense of humor been put on a shelf? When I discover how resourceful I am, I will increase my power to more fully serve others and myself.

Generosity is the willingness to give more to others than what is required. Today, I will practice being more generous with my time, resources, attention, and support. As I give more to others than what is required, I will discover how being more generous affects me, my relationships, and my surroundings.

Heroes are people we deeply admire for their special qualities. A hero may be a teacher, parent, spouse, civic leader, grandparent, spiritual mentor, activist, or friend. Today, I will think about the personal qualities of one of my leading heroes, and then I will find one of those qualities within myself to bring into my day. By using that quality, the spirit of my hero will live through me.

Kindness is as important as love, because it can be given freely to so many living things. Today, I will act in kind ways toward myself, other people, animals, plants, and the earth. Since I have an abundance of kindness within me, I will give it away at every opportunity. Through acts of kindness, I will actively nourish life.

Today, I Will...
See How I Have Improved with Age

Being sixteen years old once is enough. Today, I will notice how it is nicer to be my age than stuck forever in adolescence. I will see how I have improved with age, like a good red wine. While exploring my improvements, I will savor myself.

Many people avoid being their age. The young want to be older and the old want to be younger. Today, I will think about what makes me lucky to be my age.

Over our lifetimes, we experience the four seasons. In the spring, we are energetic and full of aspiration and hope. In the summer, we play hard and work hard to realize our dreams. In the fall, we receive the fruits of our labor and enjoy the wonders of life. In the winter, we slow down, become more patient, and cultivate wisdom. Today, I will feel blessed to be in my season. I will live in it as a gift.

We expect an old dog to nap. Today, I will realize how getting older provides me with some legitimate opportunities to take it easy. I can sit with my eyes closed for no reason, take a nice nap, go to bed early, or sleep in because, like an old dog, I can easily get away with it.

Today, I Will...
Be Proud of Who I Am

Pride is well-earned self-congratulations.
Today, I will be proud of my achievements. What
small and large accomplishments are making
me feel good about myself? Did I lend a hand to
someone or finish a project? I will acknowledge
myself today for what I have done. Feeling proud
of my accomplishments, I can say to myself, "Great
job! You are terrific!"

However small, all blades of grass have value. Today, I will recognize personal qualities whose value I take for granted. Do I fail to see the value of my patience, my curiosity, my ability to get things done without complaint, or my playful sense of humor? I will notice and celebrate the many little blades of goodness in me today.

Seeing that what we do has value makes our lives count. Today, I will explore the importance of my efforts. What large and small contributions have I made to my personal growth, the development of others, and the well-being of my community? By recognizing and understanding the value of what I do, I will discover the difference that my life has made.

A paper clip serves us by holding paper together. Today, I will consider what is holding my life together. Is it held together by my unique way of thinking, my specific beliefs, my relationships, or my work? What is my single most important anchor? By recognizing the ways it serves me, I will take a moment to honor it.

Today, I Will...
Recall Good Memories

Memory is both a great blessing and a great curse. Without memory, we cannot function. Yet when we constantly dwell on unhappy memories, they can become a curse that diminishes the quality of our lives. Today, I will take a welcome holiday from my bad memories by recalling and savoring the good times. As I do, I will discover the value of living with a more positive state of mind.

Over time, good things can disappear from us. Today, I will ponder what positive attitudes I may have lost from my childhood, teenage years, and early adulthood. Have I lost my imagination, sense of adventure, or optimism? I will choose one or two attitudes to recultivate today. By recovering what was lost, I am choosing to live more positively and powerfully.

Good memories are the past adding nice colors to the present. Today, I will recall the great people I have known, the love I have felt and received, the things I have done that were creative and adventurous, and the important goals I have achieved. By recalling those memories, I will add some beautiful colors to this day.

If we had to select one memory to live within throughout eternity, which one would we choose? Today, I will let my mind survey my memories to look for that one special memory. When I find it, I will know what I value in my life. With that knowledge, I can more consciously create what I value now.

Today, I Will...
Reject Fear

Getting in trouble is a fear we carry from childhood. Today, I will spend the whole day without that fear. This will give me access to greater freedom to be creative without fear, to speak without fear, and to think without fear. For today, I will embrace the idea that I will not be punished for living outside the lines.

Fear of failure puts the brakes on our most compelling dreams. Today, instead of thinking I might fail, I will play with the idea that any dream I pursue will come true. With that guarantee, what dream would I pursue with commitment and passion? Seeing the destination I long to reach, I will take a small step to get there today.

Often without noticing, we get tied up in knots by our fear of others who have greater status or influence. Today, I will imagine that every adult I see is a ten-year-old child. Everywhere, I will see ten-year-olds pretending to be important grownups. This will relax the hold that my fear of influential people has on me. Taking a long-overdue recess from these fears, I will get to be more spontaneous, playful, and creative.

Fear of rejection makes us hold back. Today, instead of fearing rejection, I will embrace it as a price I am willing to pay for freedom. Knowing I can accept rejection, I will express who I am as honestly as possible. Instead of wanting acceptance, I will get to be myself.

Today, I Will...
Take Risks

Most people think of taking risks as dangerous, so they naturally avoid them to protect themselves. As an alternative, consider taking risks as the willingness to stretch beyond limits in order to discover new possibilities. Today, I will take risks with my ideas, goals, and relationships. By taking risks, I will begin to live closer to the creative edge. Instead of regarding the edge as dangerous, I will think of it as the place where new discoveries can be made.

"When I" are two words that can create a conditional life; for example, "When I have enough money, I'll be happy." Today, I will think about the ways I lead a conditional life. What conditions am I putting on happiness, creativity, love, and peace of mind? What am I placing in the future that I could create right now? Seeing what I'm doing, I will quit waiting.

You can only hit a baseball by swinging the bat. Today, I will explore how much effort I put out to achieve my goals. Do I get discouraged and hesitate to try, or by overcoming my doubts, do I keep my efforts in forward motion? By discovering the value of swinging, I will see the value of trying.

Routines make ruts and take away our options. Today, I will notice my routines and look for options. What is one little thing I could alter in my morning, daytime, and evening routines that would make my day more interesting? Seeing some new choices, I will be a habit breaker today.

Today, I Will...
Tap into My Creativity

A blank page is an opportunity for creativity that can also scare us. Today, I will see new opportunities for my creativity. Instead of fearing them and doubting myself, I will feel the adventure and excitement of starting something new.

Every day starts with a new canvas. Today, I will look for ways to be creative in how I think, feel about myself, and interact with others. I will be like a young child painting with inspiration and without worry. I will use bold colors and be unafraid of expressing myself. I will paint a new canvas with the knowledge that my life is art.

We can dream up many creative uses for a common paper bag if we use our imagination. Today, I will use my imagination to dream up new ways of using myself. Could I be the spark that lights someone's creative fire? The water that puts out a fiery conflict? Instead of behaving in the same old way, I will invent a new creative use for myself today.

Creativity can become frozen by pessimistic thoughts about the future. Today, I will become aware of negative thoughts I hold about my future that undermine my creative momentum. How do those thoughts make me too tentative about my ideas, plans, and actions? Living only in the present today, I will set my doubts aside and accelerate my creative efforts.

Today, I Will...
Revise My Life Story

We become who we say we are. Today, I will
begin to revise the story I tell about myself with the
idea of achieving greater contentment, happiness,
and effectiveness. What parts of my old identity
story will I throw out? What new parts will I add?
By changing the story of who I am, I will shape who
I become.

The stories we tell about ourselves and our lives have consequences. If we create a positive story, our lives are apt to be positive, whereas a negative story will tend to produce an unhappy and diminished life. Today, I will examine the parts of my story that nourish or undermine me. Knowing I am the author of my own story, I will rewrite it. Through revision, I will set out to renew myself and my life.

Boundaries are often places where opportunities for personal growth await. Today, I will think about the boundaries I set for myself that may be holding me back from trying new things. What will it take for me to move into action? To start a new adventure today, I will push through a barrier.

Making one small change in the way we think and behave can produce big results over the long term. Today, I will choose a small thing I want to change. Will I make a slight change in the way I think about myself, make a little alteration in how I treat myself and others, or change one little thing in my plans for the future? By taking one small step in a positive direction, I will set in motion a chain of events that will change me and improve my life.

Today, I Will...
Learn Something

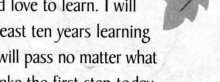

You can teach an old dog a new trick, but it will take longer. Today, I will discover one new thing I would love to learn. I will imagine spending at least ten years learning it. Knowing that time will pass no matter what I do, I might as well take the first step today.

Attention to learning accelerates personal change. Today, I will explore what I need to learn about myself and my life so I can be happier, more contented, and more creative. Do I need to learn more about my thoughts, dreams, or personal gifts? By learning more, I will nourish change.

Asking questions is one way we learn. Today, I will make my life into a school by asking questions of people who can educate me. Instead of holding back my questions for fear of looking stupid, I will forge ahead with them. By asking questions freely, I will discover how much fun it is to learn.

A river changes course because of obstacles in its way. Today, I will explore the obstacles in my way that may be calling for a change of direction in my life. What stands in my way that could become my teacher? By seeing the possibility of a new course, I will discover how to improve my life.

Today, I Will...
Ask for Help

Not wanting to look and feel needy, we often fail to ask for what we need. Today, taking a new approach, I get to ask for help. If I need caring support, I will ask for it. If I need to be heard, I will ask for it. If I need a hug, I will ask for it. I have permission to take care of myself today.

We improve our chances of making a change by seeking the help of others. Today, I will ask a friend to help me make a specific change in myself or my life. I will seek support and encouragement, and I will ask that I be held accountable for my promise. Knowing my friend is behind me, I will start making the change.

In a heavy rainstorm, it is a good idea to seek shelter. Today, I will explore where I seek cover during life storms. Do I seek shelter in a good book, a friendship, a coffee shop, or a sacred spot in nature? I will honor my sanctuaries today with feelings of thanks.

"Angels" are people who nourish, encourage, and support the lives of others. Today, I will become aware of the angels in my life by noticing who is nourishing, encouraging, and supporting me. I will write or make a call to my angels to express my thanks for what they contribute to my life. If I am acting as an angel for someone, I will also appreciate myself.

Today, I Will...
Pursue My Dreams

Our dreams come true because we actively pursue them. Today, I will recall a goal I have dreamt of pursuing that has been all talk and no action. Have I always wanted to play a musical instrument, take up art, write a book, or go on a backpacking trip? Instead of just talking, I will act.

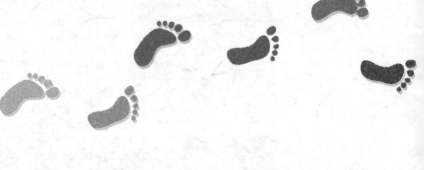

There are people who actively discourage themselves and others from pursuing their dreams. Today, I will think about whether I am one of these dream wreckers. Do I hold myself back from seeking the fulfillment of my dreams? Do I actively discourage others from pursuing their dreams? If I am a dream wrecker, what will I change?

In terms of success, luck is never as reliable as determination. Today, I will consider the strength of my determination to succeed. Where is it resolute, halfhearted, or weak? What steps could I take to strengthen it? Seeing how to bolster my determination, I will not have to rely on luck.

We do not know what we are capable of achieving until we decide to really try. Today, I will consider an important realm of my life where I am not trying hard enough. What could I achieve if I really put my heart into it? What specific things could I do to put forth more effort? How will I keep my effort going? By trying harder, I will increase my chances of making a dream come true.

Today, I Will...
Be Kind to Myself

When we are kind and considerate toward ourselves, we are more likely to be kind and considerate toward others. Today, I will be kind to myself by treating myself especially well, by acknowledging my value as a person, and by taking the extra time to satisfy my needs and desires. By being kinder and more considerate to myself, I will see the great value of taking better care of myself.

When we enjoy our own company, we feel less needy for the company of others. Today, I will look for things that I like about myself. Am I curious? Funny? A good listener? Caring? Which of my qualities make me fond of myself? Seeing those qualities, I will start savoring the time I get to spend with me.

Who needs other people's criticisms when we do such a thorough job of criticizing ourselves? Today, I will notice when I am too hard on myself and how it affects my thinking, emotions, confidence, and relationships. When I catch myself in a "put-down," I will put a stop to it by acknowledging my gifts and what I like about myself. By quieting the voice of my inner critic, I will hear from the part of me who is my advocate.

A best friend is someone we can rely on for affection, support, appreciation, and caring. Today, I will think of ways to be a better friend to myself. How could I more fully like myself, support myself, appreciate myself, and patiently care for myself? As I become a better friend to myself, I will create an unshakable inner strength.

Today, I Will...
Not Take Things Personally

We suffer from taking things too personally. Today, I will have the power to be unaffected by the critical words and inconsiderate actions of others. By not taking things personally, I will become like the lotus flower that rises in elegant beauty above the polluted water.

Most people have a hard time handling criticism. Today, I will explore how I react to criticisms that I receive about myself, my work, and how I live. Do I respond with anger or defensiveness? Do I counterattack? Do I quit listening? By noticing how I react, I will try listening to feedback with a more receptive mind so I can be more open to ideas for learning and change.

Competition can take over our lives in sneaky ways. Feeling envy toward others, wanting to be right, and seeking an advantage are signs that we are playing the competitive game. Today, I will notice when my main motive is scoring points in the game and how it influences what I do and how I do it. When I notice competition running me, I will step back and watch others compete with a feeling of detachment.

People's words do not have to hurt us. Today, I will play with the idea that I am a sieve. What others say, which might have hurt me yesterday, will pass through me without touching my heart. Instead of getting upset, I will remember that I am a good, bright, and likable person. Knowing my value, I will be able to listen without falling apart.

Today, I Will...
Nurture Community

Building communities is a form of public art.
It arises from the desire of people to have deeper
and more harmonious relationships with each other.
Today, I will consider how I could become more of
a catalyst for creating this unique art form, perhaps
within my family, school, neighborhood, place of
worship, or among my coworkers and friends. I
will become an artist of community.

Thoughtfulness is to friendship as sunshine is to a garden. Today, I will do at least one thoughtful thing for a friend. Maybe I will write my friend a note of appreciation, make a cheerful card with my own hand using felt-tip pens, take my friend to lunch, or stop by to say "Thanks for being my friend." I will cultivate friendship as if I were a bright ray of sunshine helping a delicate rosebud to bloom.

Possibilities for making change are everywhere. Today, I will notice opportunities for treating others better. This will make me aware of people I might be treating poorly. I will put myself in their shoes and their struggles. With greater empathy, I will reach out to them in new ways.

Noticing what others need from us provides many opportunities for gift giving. Today, I will pay attention to the needs of others. Do they need a gift of support, listening, compassion, or assistance? As I give my gifts to people today, I will feel and enjoy the pleasure of giving.

Today, I Will...
Communicate and Listen with Compassion

When we communicate deeply, others are more likely to understand us. Today, I will practice communicating deeply about an issue with a person I need to fully understand me. I will state the facts of the situation as I see them, then I will honestly express my feelings, needs, and what I hope will change. By choosing to communicate more deeply, I will be taking responsibility for creating the empathy and understanding I long for in my relationships.

When an alarm goes off, we react automatically without thinking. Today, I will think about my mental alarms — what sets them off and how I automatically respond when they do. Does an alarm go off in my mind when I am insensitive to others or someone else is insensitive to me? By discovering how my inner alarms set me off, I will be in a better position to turn them off.

Listening deeply helps us to more fully understand and feel greater compassion for each other. Today, I will listen for the feelings, needs, and desires of others. By listening at those deeper levels, I will understand people more completely. With clearer understanding, I will taste the sweetness of compassion.

Criticism has a difficult time existing in the company of compassionate understanding. Today, I will consider where I can offer more compassionate understanding so the volume of my criticisms can be turned down. How could I offer this as a gift to myself? How could I give it to others? By experiencing more compassion, I will get to see and feel differently.

Today, I Will...
Let Go and Forgive

Some of us long for the good times in our past and we resist accepting our present circumstances. Today, as I embrace my life as it is, I will notice how I am still hoping that my life returns to the way it was. With that awareness, I will realize that not all the good times can be recovered. This will allow me to put the past in the past so I can embrace and more fully enjoy my life as it is now.

To keep a plant blooming, a good gardener snips off spent flowers. Today, I will see what I am holding on to from my past that, while beautiful at one time, is now like a wilted flower. I will snip off one spent memory so a new bud can appear.

Forgiveness allows us to live in the present and into the future rather than living in the past. Today, I will try to forgive the people who hurt me. I will forgive myself for the pain I have caused others. As much as possible, I will clean away my resentment and guilt so the weight of my past is not such a big burden to carry.

"This too shall pass" is ancient wisdom. Today, I will apply this wisdom to any issue that disturbs me, any confusion that troubles me, and any block that stops me. I will see all problems as transient. From this awareness, a glimmer of hope will emerge.

Today, I Will...
Prevent Problems

Seeing the future can help us change the present. Today, I will see the long-term effects of my current lifestyle. Where is my life out of balance? What am I overdoing or underdoing? If I continue to live as I am, what are the consequences I might face in the future? To make a change, what would I need to add, cut back, or cut out of my life to create more balance? Seeing how the present will shape my future, I get to make some adjustments now.

Using sunscreen helps produce a healthier life. Today, I will explore how well my prevention abilities are working. Where am I preventing problems from emerging in my life? What situations are calling for greater prevention? By increasing my prevention efforts, I will improve my chances of having a better life.

It is wise to run when in the way of a falling tree. Today, I will notice where in my life I may be vulnerable to being hit by the problems of others. Seeing the potential hazards, I will quickly step out of harm's way. Other people can handle their own problems today while I try to deal with mine.

Many people think conflicts are bad, yet they can be great opportunities for growth and change. Today, I will view my conflicts from this new perspective. What are they telling me about myself and what I need to change? What specifically will I do to heed their advice? I will learn today that my conflicts can be helpful teachers showing me another way to live and be.

Today, I Will...
Examine My Life Direction

You can often see something more clearly by standing back from it. Today, I will stand at a distance from my life and explore it. This will give me a chance to appreciate what I have accomplished and what I have yet to accomplish. By seeing my life at a distance, I will become much clearer about what to do next.

"Stop and think" is a simple piece of useful wisdom. Today, I am going to stop and think. What have I been rushing through without careful reflection? What have I said and done without any concern for the consequences? As I stop and think, I will reassess my life with a bit more wisdom.

Enlightenment occurs when we suddenly wake up to see what is true. Today, I will notice where I am asleep in my thinking and my life, and then I will wake myself up by creating my own realizations. How will my insights affect how I am thinking, living, and being? By waking up to the truth about myself and my life, I will enlighten myself today.

A successful investor learns to invest in the right things. Today, I will explore my life investments. Where am I putting my time and energy? Am I investing them wisely or foolishly? Where are my prospects for a good return promising, a long shot, or pretty dismal? Seeing the potential of my various life investments, I will alter my portfolio today.

Today, I Will...
Be Flexible

When hard ground is broken up with a good shovel, something of value can grow in it. Today, I will explore one aspect of my thinking that has become so hardened it undermines my capacity to be flexible, creative, and happy. Have I placed such extreme demands on myself that they work against my well-being? Have my goals become so rigid that I fail to imagine new possibilities? By loosening up my thinking, I will be preparing myself for new opportunities to grow.

A good ball is one that bounces back easily. Today, I will explore my capacity for resilience. How well do I bounce back from disappointment, mistakes, or anger? Where I fail to bounce back quickly, I will wonder why. This awareness will give me a good chance to improve my responses to setbacks.

Compulsions are where we have quit making choices. Today, I will notice where in my life I am compelled and have lost my freedom to choose. Am I driven to work, argue, organize, impress others, or get my way? Seeing where I have lost my freedom, I will reestablish my power to choose.

Flexibility is one of the greatest personal gifts. Today, I will create a more flexible state of mind. I will be receptive to perspectives other than my own. I will seek new avenues of thought and action, rather than staying on old, well-trodden paths. I will be like a young tree whose flexibility allows it to bend easily in the face of strong winds.

Today, I Will...
Cultivate Wisdom

Wisdom emerges when we actively cultivate it. Today, I will seek wisdom as I address the many issues of my life and my immediate circumstances. If I become upset or discouraged, I will seek wise ways of addressing and changing my feelings. If difficult problems arise during the day, I will actively create wise solutions. Wisdom will be my goal today.

We live in mind boxes and fail to notice the loss of adventure. Today, I will think about the size of my mind box. What limitations am I placing on myself? How could I expand the size of my mind so there is more room to create novel ideas in my work, relationships, and life? With more freedom to innovate, my capacity to be more adventurous will expand.

Our five senses are some of our best learning tools. Today, I will appreciate my senses for what they teach me. What do I learn from sight, smell, touch, taste, and hearing? How do my senses work together to serve me so well? By appreciating my senses, I will celebrate one of the miracles of being human.

The questions we ask ourselves and others guide and therefore influence the activity of the mind. Today, I will become more keenly aware of my questions. I will consciously choose questions that awaken the spirit of creativity, wisdom, and connection. By choosing my questions with care, I will cultivate a fascinating day.

Today, I Will...
Choose My Thoughts Carefully

We cannot control what people say and do to us, but we can control our thinking and how we respond. Today, I will manage my thinking so my responses to others are not just automatic reactions but are what I choose. By exercising the power to manage my reactions, I will create a new way to be in relationships.

A good gardener will nurture healthy roots. Today, I will explore my positive thoughts as if they were roots sending me much-needed nourishment. I will become aware of thoughts that support my creativity, peace of mind, and happiness. Then I will seek to strengthen those thoughts so I can create a more abundant and enjoyable life.

Persistent whining drains our creative energy and makes us ineffective. Today, I will consider whether I am a persistent whiner and how my constant complaining affects me and others. By seeing the negative effects of my whining, I will change what I am doing. I will turn off my whining machine and turn my complaints into positive requests for change.

A happy life arises naturally when we cultivate a happy mind. Today, by making one small positive change in my thinking, I will create the power to elevate my happiness and the happiness of others. By planting a few happy thoughts in my mind, my life will become happier.

Today, I Will...
Seek Balance

It is easy to push over a person who is standing on one leg. Today, I will consider where I am feeling out of balance. Is it an image issue? Is my thinking out of whack? Is my behavior too intense or too tame? By realizing what I need to balance, I will be able to live in greater harmony and stability.

"Both" is a balancing word. Today, I will notice how often I think "either/or" while making decisions. How would my thinking change if instead of "either/or" I thought "both"? By seeking the midpoint between seemingly contradictory options, I will try to create greater balance in my thinking and my actions.

When we achieve inner balance, we can apply less force to achieve good results. Today, I will notice where I am using too much force. Am I too pushy when promoting myself and my ideas? Am I applying too much control in my relationships? Seeing where I am applying too much force, I can ease up and not push so hard. In better balance, I will seek results with harmony in mind.

A personal "weakness" can be a strength and a "strength," if taken to an extreme, can become a weakness. Today, I will explore these two sides of my nature. What strengths grow out of my weaknesses? What weaknesses do my strengths create? I will also consider today how my weaknesses and strengths work together to make me a more balanced person.

Today, I Will...
Love Myself

We are less important than we would like to be, but also far more special than we realize. Today, I will think about my place in the universe. I will see how very small I am in that vastness; then I will realize that there will never be another person like me in the universe, ever. This awareness will make me feel humble and very special.

No one said life would be a piece of cake. Today, I will honor myself for getting through the tough times. I will think about the resources I used successfully to get through them. Did I draw on my patience, creativity, stoic acceptance, or courage? With those resources clearly in mind, I will consider how I might be using them more effectively in my life now. I will strive to be more "resource-full" today.

We constantly compare ourselves to others and then feel inadequate when we fail to measure up. Today, instead of worrying about how I measure up, I will think and behave in ways that cheer me up. I am going to turn up my inner light so I can clearly see and enjoy this day.

The four little paths to personal freedom are simple. Live as if you have nothing to prove, nothing to defend, nothing to gain, and nothing to hide. Today, I will tread these four little paths to experience the freedom of fully being and loving myself.

Today, I Will...
Create My Ideal Day

A "perfect day" can be created. Today, I will dream up my perfect day. I will include activities that make me happy, contented, relaxed, and fulfilled. When my dream day is designed, I will set the date when I will make it come true.

Hope is the willingness to imagine the future as a bright possibility. Today, I will live in the hope that things will get better for me, my loved ones, and the world. Hope will nourish my spirit today so I can look toward the future with positive expectations.

Having the gift of life makes every day a blessing. Today, I will make this day a blessing by choosing how I will think, speak, interact, and create. I will make this day into a gift for myself to celebrate the fact that I am alive.

You will never gain weight by having sweet thoughts. Today, I will devour sweet thoughts. What is sweet about my life? How are my friends sweet? What makes me sweet? Let's face it. This is going to be a sweet day.

Today, I Will...
Thrive

Where the soil is richest, plants will easily grow and thrive. Today, I will explore areas within myself where I am most prepared for cultivation. What parts of me are fertile for change and growth? Is there a particularly rich opportunity? What are the steps I will take to cultivate it? By nourishing my development in this way, I will be a life gardener today.